This Anguishing Blessed Journey

A Mother's Faith Journal through Autism

Sonya Shafer

This Anguishing Blessed Journey
by Sonya Shafer

Printed in the United States of America

ISBN 1-594670-80-3

The following Scriptures are taken from the King James Version: Psalm 16:11; Psalm 37:5; Proverbs 16:3; Mark 9:24; John 10:10; Philippians 4:13; 1 John 4:19.

Xulon Press
www.XulonPress.com

Xulon Press books are available in bookstores everywhere, and on the Web at www.XulonPress.com.

To Hannah,

May you grow in your faith

as much as

you've helped me to grow in mine.

Introduction

When we diagnosed my youngest daughter with autism spectrum disorder, I found two kinds of books available: personal stories and practical therapies. Both were helpful, but I found nothing that addressed the spiritual abyss we parents can fall into when the diagnosis sinks in.

As it happened, the Lord engineered circumstances so that I was reading through the entire Bible during that first year of the diagnosis. As He began to bring comfort to my aching heart and peace to my grieving spirit, I started to write down what He was showing me. This faith journal shares the

- heartfelt prayers,
- gentle, loving Biblical truths,
- everyday spiritual insights,
- anguishing emotional struggles, and
- blessed strength from Scripture

that all played a part in my spiritual journey that first year, a journey that was both anguishing and blessed.

"Isn't *anguishing* a rather strong word?" a friend asked.

"Yes, it is," I replied. "But I can't find a better word to describe that gut-wrenching pain I feel whenever I think about one of my children being harmed in any way. I actually thought about calling the book *This Anguish of My Soul*, from Isaiah 38:15, but that title wouldn't convey a complete picture. The journey has not been without its blessings."

I've come to know God more intimately because I needed Him so desperately. I've learned compassion for the weak and respect for those who minister to them. I've watched my other children grow in grace and patience, and I've discovered they have abilities that I hadn't seen before. I've shared in the comfort that comes from the fellowship of believers, brothers and sisters in Christ. I've gained strength from some wonderful Christian ladies all over the world who are walking their own journeys mingled with anguish and blessing.

If you are a mother who has asked, "Will I ever stop crying?" then you understand the word "anguish." But be assured that this journey is also blessed. Let your suffering nudge you closer to the Savior. Run to Him and find the comfort and healing that He can bring to your grieving heart.

"Praise be to the God and Father of our Lord Jesus Christ, the Father of compassion and the God of all comfort, who comforts us in all our troubles, so that we can comfort those in any trouble with the comfort we ourselves have received from God" (2 Corinthians 1:3, 4).

Day 1, morning

It's Mother's Day, and we are embarking on an adventure with Hannah. As we've been researching the past few months, we have determined that Hannah is exhibiting autistic symptoms:

- She won't look us in the eye.
- She plays in her own little world, oblivious to what is happening around her.
- She lies on her bed for hours, looking at a toy.
- She doesn't play pretend.
- She doesn't acknowledge people coming or going around her.
- She doesn't respond when we call her name.
- She's losing her speech and language.
- Instead of talking to us, she just recites lines from computer programs and cassette tapes (called "delayed echolalia") sometimes at applicable moments, but most often not on topic.
- She lines up blocks, books, puzzles, or toys, instead of playing with them.
- She doesn't look at the book I'm reading to her; she plays with her own book or toy instead.
- She doesn't point to anything.

- She doesn't look at something we point to; she looks at our fingers instead.
- She has sporadic outbursts of "no, no, no" for unknown reasons.
- She stands still for hugs, but doesn't open her arms to return them.
- She looks at her plate during meal times or sits with her arm over her face.
- She grabs our hands to pull us to what she wants.
- She continually repeats a sequence in playing.
- She's fascinated with lights and ceiling fans.
- She's entranced with fire. (For several days leading up to her fourth birthday, she was singing, "Happy Birthday to you, now blow out the candles." At her birthday, she sat staring at the flames and wouldn't respond to our encouragement to blow out the candles. After the flames were extinguished, she returned to singing and reciting the phrases.)
- She uses a high-pitched voice to resist when challenged.

We believe God has led us to a possibly helpful tool and are planning to begin one-on-one intensive training sessions with her tomorrow.

Joshua 1:9 has become a source of strength as we stand on the verge of a long battle in unknown territory (just like Joshua):

> "Be strong and courageous. Do not be terrified; do not be discouraged, for the LORD your God will be with you wherever you go."

There's a big difference between having the Lord point down a path and say, "Go that way" and having the Lord take your hand in His and say, "Here's the path; let's walk it together"—the Lord your God will be with you!

Day 1, afternoon

In my spirit I'm anticipating a spiritual battle over Hannah. I feel a little akin to the parents who fell at Jesus' feet and begged Him to deliver their children from the evil spirits that oppressed them.

Dear Father, I pray that the name, blood, and power of Jesus will completely surround our sessions and that the enemy will be banned from interfering.

Day 1, evening

A wonderful friend called today. She always knows how to ask the right questions to get at the heart of the matter, and soon I found myself sobbing into the phone. I related my struggle with knowing I should accept this as God's will and yet breaking down in tears every day at unexpected times. She reassured me: "It is not wrong to grieve. I'm sure the Father grieves over things that, because of the curse, aren't as they should be. In fact, we're all not as we should be."

Day 2

God's grace was truly evident during our first session. It went better than we expected.

Our first drill was to get Hannah to "attend" (pay attention through eye contact). The first few tries were met with resistance and crying, but the last few tries the tears changed to smiles.

All-in-all the session was positive, and I think she'll be cooperative tomorrow when I suggest doing another session (unlike today, when she cried all the way to the room). Of course, we're learning that a response today doesn't guarantee the same response tomorrow.

Oh, Father, how patient You are with Your children!

Day 5

"With my God I can scale a wall"!!!!—2 Samuel 22:30

Our "battle cry" for our work with Hannah is STORM THE CASTLE (taken from Catherine Maurice's book "Let Me Hear Your Voice"). It seems like there is a giant wall—a fortress—between Hannah and us. But with God, we can scale that wall!

Day 6

God is graciously letting us see some of His plan unfolding. He moved us to this town two years ago—we thought because of work possibilities. But it seems that some of His plan was to put us ten minutes from a wonderful church, two doors from a mother of an autistic daughter who had the book we needed to start us on this journey with Hannah, and right next door to a lady who has a friend studying speech therapy with children with special needs. That friend arrived last night to spend a week. During that time she will also be observing Hannah and helping us determine what her needs are.

All three facets have been developing over several years, and God orchestrated them to intersect our lives right now. This has been an encouraging week.

Thank You, Father for answering our prayers for grace, wisdom, patience, and encouragement many times over.

> "Commit thy way unto the LORD; trust also in him; and he shall bring it to pass."—Psalm 37:5

He is making it clear that if we commit the way to Him and trust in Him, He will make it happen.

Day 10

God is my strength—He will strengthen me for
the journey ahead.
my fortress—He will protect me and
cover me 'round.
my loving God—He does everything for
my good.

I watch for You—Help me to not walk ahead of
You or dawdle behind You.
I sing praise to You—In faith I sing of Your
greatness and goodness to
me.
—Psalm 59:9, 17

Day 17

"Cast your cares on the LORD
and he will sustain you;
he will never let the righteous fall."—Psalm 55:22

Day 20

This week has continued with ups and downs. We're finding out how smart Hannah is—and how resistant to any attempts to challenge her. (Yes, I am a lot like that when the Father reveals something in my life that needs to be changed.)

She called John "Daddy" for the first time yesterday, so he's pumped!

Father, I wonder if that's a little glimpse into Your heart when we call You "Abba" for the first time.

God has continued to surround us with resources, people, grace, and strength at the moments we need them.

Day 22

"Who holds in his hand your life and all your ways."
—Daniel 5:23

God is gracious and merciful, and Hannah can be in no better hands than His.

Day 26

Psalm 78:57 hit me between the eyes today. It says that the Israelites were as unreliable as a faulty bow because they were disloyal and faithless. That word picture of a faulty bow reminded me of Psalm 127:4 and 5:

> "Like arrows in the hands of a warrior are sons born in one's youth. Blessed is the man whose quiver is full of them."

I've heard that verse applied to parents' preparing their children and pointing them, like arrows, in the right direction for service to God. If I am disloyal to God or faithless, I am an unreliable bow that can't be depended on to point my children in the right direction.

Lord, help me remain loyal to You and keep my faith in You through this valley. My children are watching.

Day 30

"Give me an undivided heart":

to fear God,
to praise God,
to glorify His name
—Psalm 86:11, 12

Wholehearted devotion: that's what I want to give You, Father.

I don't want to be constantly second-guessing whether to do things Your way; I want to fear You.

I don't want to keep worrying about what has happened and whether You're in control and can handle it; I want to praise You.

I really don't want to cast You in a bad light to those around me or steal the credit for what You are doing; I want to glorify Your name.

Please, give me an undivided heart.

Day 34

Father, I pray specifically for Hannah's little spirit. I haven't heard her sing a Jesus-related song in several weeks now, and I don't know what to make of it. She listens to Bible songs and praise and worship songs every day at nap and bedtimes and used to sing "Jesus Loves Me," but her singing has stopped. Help us to be very careful that in the battle for her mind, we don't overlook the battle for her soul.

Day 35

Thank You, Father, for honoring our prayers of yesterday and encouraging our hearts. Hannah sang "Jesus Loves Me" this morning!

Day 43

"My flesh and my heart may fail,
but God is the strength of my heart."—Psalm 73:26

Day 55

We continue to be surrounded by God's grace and strength. We're into the less stressful stage of "routine" now (as opposed to everything being new and requiring extra brain cells and time).

God keeps giving encouragement along the way. I had postponed teaching Hannah a couple of skills because I didn't have the supplies I needed. Today I finally ordered the materials through the Internet. When I got to the order confirmation screen, the address of the company showed up. It's about twenty minutes north of us. That was an unexpected blessing. It's also been an ongoing blessing to discover all the supplies we already have from previous years of purchases and gifts.

Thanks, Father, for orchestrating all those Christmas and birthday presents over the past twelve years!

Day 58

"At the LORD's command they encamped and at the LORD's command they set out."—Numbers 9:23

As God's people followed where He led, nothing was done by default; they sought the Lord's direction for both progress and plateaus.

Lord, direct us when to move on to teach the next skill and when to be patient and keep plugging away at the one we seem to be stuck on.

Day 59

"Six days you shall labor, but on the seventh day you shall rest; even during the plowing season and harvest you must rest."—Exodus 34:21

Plowing seasons and harvest were busy times, yet God told His people to take a day of rest in the midst of the urgent tasks staring them in the face. To stop working must have taken faith. If the people quit harvesting for a day, an unexpected hailstorm might destroy their crop before they got it all in. Yet, God's plan for a day of rest was for their good.

When God calls me aside for a time of rest, I can either rest fretfully, worrying about what isn't getting done (like Hannah's afternoon session), or I can rest gratefully, trusting God to take care of the details. Sometimes (most of the time!) my times of rest are forced upon me through interruptions—illness, change in scheduling, others' requests; sometimes I actually respond to God's still small voice calling me to "come aside and rest awhile."

Either way, Lord, help me to see each time of rest as for my good and help me to gratefully accept such times in faith.

Day 60

Two things:

God is strong;
God is loving.
—Psalm 62:11, 12

I don't have to remember a whole treatise on God in my situation. He boils it down to those two most important things. I can remember those. I can repeat them over and over throughout the circumstances of the day.

When I question our progress and wonder if Hannah will ever come back to us . . . "God is strong."

When grief overtakes me and I wonder if anyone understands . . . "God is loving."

When I feel like I can't force my feet to walk into that session room again . . . "God is strong."

When I ask *Why me?* for the hundredth time . . . "God is loving."

Day 61

"Since my youth, O God, you have taught me. . . ."
"Even when I am old and gray,
do not forsake me. . . ."
"Though you have made me see troubles,
many and bitter,
you will restore my life again."—Psalm 71:14–21

We've had a long relationship, Lord, You and I. Thank You for calling me to Yourself when I was young and for teaching Me about Yourself through all these years. Now I'm counting on You to keep walking with me through this stage of my life. Don't leave me now, Lord. Even though Your plan has included these many, bitter troubles, I trust what You've taught me about Yourself. I trust You. And I'm counting on Your promise that You will restore my life again. When? I don't know. How? I don't know. But You will.

Day 62

Today we picked blueberries. Hannah filled about one-third of a gallon bucket by herself, sorting out the white berries from the blue ones all the while. As one dear friend has observed, she seems happier now than she ever has. Something has changed about her countenance. Does she still struggle? Oh yes! Many times! But she seems to be enjoying what she has discovered about the life she was formerly distant from.

It's the same with me too, Father, isn't it? As I grow in my faith, I discover that "in thy presence is fulness of joy" (Psalm 16:11) and that Jesus came to give me life "more abundantly" (John 10:10)!

Day 69

There is always that nagging thought present: "What if she hits a brick wall and can't go any farther?"

"Lord, I believe; help thou mine unbelief." —Mark 9:24

Day 75

"I cried out to God for help;
I cried out to God to hear me.
When I was in distress, I sought the Lord;
at night I stretched out untiring hands
and my soul refused to be comforted.

I remembered you, O God, and I groaned;
I mused, and my spirit grew faint.
You kept my eyes from closing;
I was too troubled to speak.
I thought about the former days,
the years of long ago;
I remembered my songs in the night.
My heart mused and my spirit inquired:
'Will the Lord reject forever?
Will he never show his favor again?
Has his unfailing love vanished forever?
Has his promise failed for all time?
Has God forgotten to be merciful?
Has he in anger withheld his compassion?'

Then I thought, 'To this I will appeal:
the years of the right hand of the Most High.'
I will remember the deeds of the LORD;
yes, I will remember your miracles of long ago.
I will meditate on all your works
and consider all your mighty deeds.

Your ways, O God, are holy.
What god is so great as our God?
You are the God who performs miracles;
you display your power among the peoples."
—Psalm 77:1–14

Day 81

"Surely God is my help;
the Lord is the one who sustains me."— Psalm 54:4

I need Your stamina, Lord, to persevere. I'm getting tired and a bit overwhelmed with all that You've put on my plate right now. Help.

Day 97

"I cry out to God Most High,
to God, who fulfills his purpose for me."—Psalm 57:2

Lord, why is this Your purpose for me?

Day 105

"O LORD, you are my God;
I will exalt you and praise your name,
for in perfect faithfulness
you have done marvelous things,
things planned long ago."—Isaiah 25:1

This chapter in my life is no surprise to You, Lord. You planned it long ago, and I must believe that You have done it in perfect faithfulness for my good and Your glory.

Day 106

Hannah lives in her own little world, oblivious to events around her unless she is interacting with us (talking, listening, sharing the experiences). Continual prayer keeps me aware of the Father's events, what He's up to. Not praying makes me oblivious to His work; it keeps me in my own little world. I guess our Heavenly Father desires our fellowship with Him just as we desire Hannah's fellowship with us.

Day 109

"Relent, O LORD! How long will it be?
Have compassion on your servants.
Satisfy us in the morning with your unfailing love,
that we may sing for joy and be glad all our days.
Make us glad for as many days as you have afflicted us,
for as many years as we have seen trouble.
May your deeds be shown to your servants,
your splendor to their children.
May the favor of the LORD our God rest upon us;
establish the work of our hands for us—
yes, establish the work of our hands."
—Psalm 90:13–17

Probably the hardest part is the unknown factor. How long will this last? What is Hannah's potential? Will this ever change? When? Please, Lord, make us joyful again. We'll be careful to give You the credit when explaining Your works to our children. And, in the meantime, Lord, please establish all this work with Hannah. Don't let it slip away into the air; establish it like a firm foundation, like planks in a bridge to reach from her world to ours.

Day 111

When I feel like I'm slipping,
His love supports me.
When my anxiety is great,
His consolation brings joy.
—Psalm 94:18, 19

"You will keep in perfect peace
him whose mind is steadfast,
because he trusts in you."—Isaiah 26:3

Lord, help me to steadfastly trust in You and live in Your perfect peace. Keep my mind steadfast, not tossed about.

Day 125

"All that we have accomplished
You have done for us"!—Isaiah 26:12

Thank You, Jesus!

Day 127

"There are three stages in the work of God:
impossible, difficult, done."
—James Hudson Taylor

Day 130

Lord, we've been working on this skill for more than fifty days! Will she ever get it?

Then I realized that the Father must teach me some truths again and again until I truly believe and live each one, until I finally "get it." I may even "pass" one trial that tests that skill, but the Father knows when it actually becomes a part of my life, a part of my thought process.

We teach Hannah what she needs to know in incremental steps. The Father leads me one step at a time.

Day 138

Father, as an act of faith, I thank You for Hannah's autism. I do not understand how it is a good thing, but I want to honor You, obey Your will, and clear the way for You to show Your salvation in this.

"He who sacrifices thank offerings honors me,
and he prepares the way
so that I may show him the salvation of God."
—Psalm 50:23

"Give thanks in all circumstances, for this is God's will for you in Christ Jesus."—1 Thessalonians 5:18

I thank You that she is not like the other girls.

I thank You that she requires more wisdom and grace, and so I am forced to run to You more often.

Day 145

"In quietness and trust is your strength."—Isaiah 30:15

The Israelites wouldn't accept that truth; they "would have none of it."

Lord, help me find the strength that comes from being quiet before You and trusting, rather than drowning, in the turmoil of "what if's."

Day 149

When Hezekiah received a threatening letter, he took it to the temple and spread it out before the Lord as he prayed (Isaiah 37:9–15). So many times I pray in my head and in vague terms. I figure God knows what I need and knows my thoughts. But what a powerful picture of dependence on God if I follow Hezekiah's example!

I can take a physical representation of my concern and spread it out before the Lord as I pray. I can lay out Hannah's drill book and point to the specific problem and say, "This one, Lord. This is the one she's not getting."

Then the next time I see that drill book during her session, I'll be reminded of its being covered over in prayer. I won't look at it the same way again. It will be a physical memorial of casting those cares on the Lord.

Day 157

> "But what can I say?
> He has spoken to me, and he himself has done this.
> I will walk humbly all my years because of this
> anguish of my soul."
> —Isaiah 38:15

Yes, Lord, You are teaching me humility and compassion because of this anguish of my soul.

Day 159

In a note from my mom:
"Sometimes the best worship
comes from a broken heart."

Day 165

> "Even to your old age and gray hairs I am he,
> I am he who will sustain you.
> I have made you and I will carry you;
> I will sustain you and I will rescue you."
> —Isaiah 46:4

Father, You know me better than anybody else, even better than I know myself, because You made me. You know what I need every minute of every day. And You have promised to sustain me, even to carry me when I don't have any strength left, and to rescue me. And that promise is good for the rest of my life. I'm leaning on You, Father, because I'm weary.

Day 169

I wonder sometimes how our adventure with Hannah affects our other children. So much of our time and effort are being poured into our youngest that I'm certain there are times when the others feel slighted, put off.

Lord, You know my heart. You know I don't want any of my children to suffer. Yet it is in the trials and suffering that we grow stronger in our faith. Thank You that, as one friend put it, the children are learning valuable lessons about self-sacrifice and compassion and responsibility during this season in our family's life.

Day 175

Knowing what God wants (His will) for my life brings:

the ability to live worthy of His calling
the ability to please Him (which can only be done with faith—Hebrews 11:6)
the ability to bear fruit
growth, knowing Him better
strength
endurance
patience
joyful thanks
—Colossians 1:9–12

Lord, I don't understand, but this is what You have planned for my life right now—this is Your will. Only through embracing it will I gain the endurance, strength, and patience that I need to bear fruit in it. Help me to please You by accepting Your will in faith and to live worthy of Your high calling. Thank You for the privilege of being Your child.

Day 183

Today in church our pastor challenged us to think about where we were investing our lives. He asked, "What are you working for that money cannot buy and death cannot take away?" Hannah's development cannot be bought with money, and going to the arms of the Savior through the doorway of death would only fulfill our quest by giving her a whole, complete mind. Her progress is a worthy investment of our lives.

Day 190

Jeremiah 9:23, 24—

Not boast in our wisdom, strength, or riches

Boast that we understand and know God

Who exercises kindness, justice, and righteousness

Lord, any success or progress that we have achieved cannot be credited to

our own wisdom to find the right resources or

our own strength to carry through on the therapy or

our money to buy what we need.

Our only "claim to fame" is that we know YOU: the God Who is kind and just and right. Thank You for the progress You've given us.

Day 200

"Cursed is the one who trusts in man. . . ."
"Blessed is the man who trusts in the LORD,
whose confidence is in him.
He will be like a tree planted by the water
that sends out its roots by the stream.
It does not fear when heat comes;
its leaves are always green.
It has no worries in a year of drought
and never fails to bear fruit."—Jeremiah 17:5–8

Confidence and trust in God produces
(1) deep roots that both sustain and stabilize me;
(2) no fear of heat—I can face without fear the trials that refine my faith (1 Peter 1:7);
(3) leaves that are always green—The fact that, by God's grace, I am not "withering away" is a witness to others and a refreshing shade to those nearby;
(4) no worries in drought—My trust in Him provides the nourishment I need during ongoing trials when it seems that He is far away;
(5) the certainty of bearing fruit—I will see a lasting result.

Day 218

We had a baby dedication at church this morning—a beautiful little girl—and I cried. At unexpected times the grief overwhelms me; the loss of the "perfect" child that I thought I had. For close to four years we were operating under the thought that she was just like the other three: smart, quick, creative, eager to learn. Since May I have been hit between the eyes that that child is gone. Yes, she is smart in her own way, but not in the way I held close to my heart for those four years.

Little things will expose the grief and prompt the tears. We'll be singing and clapping hands in church, and I'll look over at her sitting in her chair with downcast eyes; and I wonder, "Will she ever clap her hands to the music? Will she ever sing along with other believers in corporate worship? Will she ever come to an understanding of trust in Jesus?" A friend will announce a wedding, and I'll wonder, "Will she ever be able to run a household? Will she ever be able to care for children? Will she even understand the changes her body will go through?"

True, some of those thoughts are from the enemy, and I must constantly turn them back over to God so they don't become anxious thoughts, but they still cause pain to my mommy heart.

It's probably a good thing that I haven't played the piano since May. I sat down last night to try to find a song that I could play in church and couldn't make it through any of them without crying. I think expressing myself musically is just too emotional right now.

Day 219

Advice from a dear friend who has her own ongoing trial:

1) "From Dr. Tony Evans I gathered that when I have a problem, I need to redirect my thoughts to all of the things for which I should be thankful."

2) "From our study of Martin Luther I learned that Satan hates joyful music. So when you quit playing the piano, he wins. I would recommend that you play the piano MORE."

3) "It might help to focus on smaller goals. Our friend bought a house that needs to be completely remodeled. He is so overwhelmed with the enormity of the task that he has not accomplished much at all in the six months that they have been living in the house. Rather, he should focus on making one room at a time livable. So rather than focusing today on making Hannah a beautiful woman/bride/mother . . . maybe make smaller goals. Look: She's smiling, etc."

"You are running a long race, and you don't want to run out of stamina."

Day 235

"I can do all things through Christ
which strengtheneth me."—Philippians 4:13

*"God never gives strength for tomorrow
or for the next hour,
but only for the strain of the minute."
—Oswald Chambers,
My Utmost for His Highest*

Day 242

"Commit thy works unto the LORD and thy thoughts shall be established."—Proverbs 16:3

It's easy to flit here and there wondering (worrying, really) about what we are doing or need to be doing with Hannah. Father, I commit our work to You, trusting You to lead us to what we need to be doing—just as You've so faithfully led us in the past. Please establish my thoughts to focus on what You have revealed instead of what You have not revealed right now.

Day 258

At lunch today Hannah was fascinated with eating the crumbs off her plate one by one, while ignoring the big slice of pound cake sitting there. The Spirit reminded me how I am often content to eat the little crumbs of hope that others throw my way instead of going directly to the source—God. He offers me a big, unending slice of grace and hope, but I blindly wait for some secondhand crumbs to fall my way.

Open my eyes, Lord; I want to see Jesus.

Day 263

"And I will give them a heart to know me,
that I am the LORD."—Jeremiah 24:7

Father, You know that more than anything else I want Hannah to have a heart for God, to love You with all her heart, soul, mind, and strength. Please, please give her a heart to know You.

Day 277

"God does not expect us to work for Him, but to work with Him."
—Oswald Chambers, *If You Will Ask*

Once there was a king who had a very special child, a child who needed extra care. The king could not entrust this child to just any of his subjects to raise; he searched for a couple who had already proven faithful to him and who, he knew, would raise the child after his own heart. He lovingly placed the child in their home and reassured them that he was available to help them anytime, day or night.

"I thank Christ Jesus our Lord, who has given me strength, that he considered me faithful, appointing me to his service."—1 Timothy 1:12

Day 280

"Let us not become weary in doing good, for at the proper time we will reap a harvest if we do not give up."
—Galatians 6:9

Lord, I'm tired of listening to the continual echoing. I'm weary of doing the same drill for the 143rd time. I'm tired of hearing the repeated phrases and wondering whether to reply (again) or ignore. I'm tired of wracking my brain to figure out how to get her to keep her mouth open when I brush her teeth. I'm discouraged at the bad day that came right after a series of good, hope-filled days. I'm tired of being the referee between she and her sisters. I'm weary of the struggle; I'm losing heart in the midst of the battle. Don't let me give up, Lord!

Day 290

"But thou art making me, I thank Thee, sire.
What Thou hast done and doest Thou knowest
well.
And I will help Thee; gently in Thy fire
I will lie burning; on Thy potter's wheel
I will whirl patiently, though my brain should
reel.
Thy grace shall be enough the grief to quell,
And growing strength perfect through weakness
dire."
—George MacDonald

I do feel like I'm whirling, Father (Sire). But I want to cooperate as You mold me into the vessel You have designed, even if it is painful. I want to lie gently in Your fire; I want to whirl patiently on Your potter's wheel. Please pour on the grace and strength, because I need it!

Day 297

"We love him, because he first loved us."—1 John 4:19

Before we ever said, "Lord, I love You," He was saying, "I love you." True love loves a person even though she may never express love back.

Day 300

"Look to the Lord and his strength;
seek his face always."—Psalm 105:4

Day 312

The thought occurred to me today—if this is God's will for me, then it is also God's will for the other children in our family. I don't have to pray that God will somehow keep them from being scarred by this valley we're walking through. It's not a matter of God somehow salvaging the broken pieces and trying to make something good out of it; instead God has purposely included this valley to shape their lives for what He has planned in their futures. The experiences they go through growing up with an autistic sister are not an unfortunate accident; they are journeying through God's intentional training ground—holy ground.

God is not against us.
God is not neutral toward us.
GOD IS FOR US!
—Romans 8:31

Day 315

"My splendor is gone
    and all that I had hoped from the LORD.
I remember my affliction and my wandering,
    the bitterness and the gall.
I well remember them,
    and my soul is downcast within me.
Yet this I call to mind
    and therefore I have hope:
Because of the LORD's great love we are not consumed,
    for his compassions never fail.
They are new every morning;
    great is your faithfulness.
I say to myself, 'The LORD is my portion;
    therefore I will wait for him.'
The LORD is good to those whose hope is in him,
    to the one who seeks him;
it is good to wait quietly
    for the salvation of the LORD.
Though he brings grief, he will show compassion,
    so great is his unfailing love.
For he does not willingly bring affliction
    or grief to the children of men."
—Lamentations 3:18–26, 32, 33

Day 324

Yesterday I was reading a chapter of "Prince Caspian," one of the Narnia books, to one of the girls. Hannah came into the room and wanted us to help her with the computer. I told her we would help after we finished reading. She decided to climb up on the bed with us and wait. She sat there for a good two or three pages. We were reading the part where Lucy wakes up, sees Aslan, and he tells her to wake the others and follow him. Lucy encounters all kinds of skepticism and sulky attitudes as she tries to wake the others and convince them that Aslan is waiting to lead them to safety. Aslan had warned her that the others would not be able to see him at first, so most of their arguments are to that point.

So, you have the picture: I'm reading aloud several pages from a story with no pictures, written in C.S. Lewis's classic style. Two sentences from the end, Hannah looked up and said, "Oh, they want to see the lion."

Even more than an academic significance, this represents to me a spiritual reassurance that Jesus is "in there" with Hannah. I think He prompted her to say that to confirm to me that He is working in her heart and she is not alone. I have no explanation from a physical development standpoint: we've been working for days on giving one-sentence stories with pictures, and she hasn't even been able to answer the obvious "Who?" questions. The only explanation I can give is a spiritual miracle given from the loving hands of the Lion of Judah, the Lord Jesus Christ.

Day 338

OK, Lord, I'll admit that I'm afraid. I'm afraid of what might happen. I'm afraid of what might not happen. I'm afraid that I'll spend all this time and effort on the child you have entrusted to me and end up with nothing better, maybe something worse.

Now I think I understand that servant in Matthew 25:14–30 who simply buried the talent that his master had entrusted to him. I never before understood his reasoning:

> "I knew that you are a hard man, harvesting where you have not sown and gathering where you have not scattered seed. So I was afraid and went out and hid your talent in the ground."

Now I understand that there were no guarantees. He could have lost everything in his possession; he had no promise of success. No wonder he was afraid.

I know, Lord, that You are giving me no guarantee of "success." Looking at it from a human point of view, You may seem hard because Your ways are not our ways. Your way might decree that Hannah not progress past a certain point. Your way might include her getting worse; I don't know.

But I don't want to look at it from a human point of view! I want to get to the place where a guarantee is not important to me, where faithfulness is my only desire and standard of measuring success. I want to hear you say, "Well done, good and faithful servant!" Help me to wholeheartedly work with what You've given me, not fearing the outcome. Help me to be faithful.

Day 351

In a recent e-mail I was sharing with a friend about my tendency to look ahead at all that we have yet to accomplish instead of looking back at how far we've come. She asked whether I had a videotape of Hannah's first session that might encourage me to focus on the progress we've made.

Many people recommended that I videotape Hannah to document her progress over the months, but somehow I could never bring myself to do it. I think I just don't want to remember what things were like back then; I don't want to remember her that way.

"Forgetting what is behind and straining toward what is ahead, I press on toward the goal."—Philippians 3:13, 14

Day 357

Today we were at the rubber stamp store. I was holding Hannah's hand to keep her near me. She let go for a minute to readjust the stuffed animal that she was holding in her other hand. Then the BEST thing happened: she looked up at me, smiled, and reached for my hand again! I can't remember her ever reaching to hold my hand; I've always reached for hers. Of course, I teared up right there in the store!

A little thing to most moms; a big thing to me. Thank You, Lord, for little big things!

Day 359

A friend sang this song in church. I think it was chosen by God directly for me, for this is my prayer as I come to the end of this first year of our journey with autism. I want to go willingly down this path to the places where God's glory has not yet been known. Who knows how He will bring glory to Himself through Hannah's life in the years ahead? I certainly don't know; but I want to follow Him so I can be there to see it! I want to embrace this journey—not reluctantly drag my feet and grumble all the way; I want to make this journey my home, for it is hand-designed by my loving Father.

I Will Go

Give me ears to hear Your Spirit;
give me feet to follow through.
Give me hands to touch the hurting
and the faith to follow You.

Give me grace to be a servant;
give me mercy for the lost.
Give me passion for Your glory,
give me passion for the cross.

And I will go where there are no easy roads,
leave the comforts that I know.
I will go and let this journey be my home.
I will go. I will go.

I'll let go of my ambition,
cut the roots that run too deep.
I will learn to give away
what I cannot really keep,
what I cannot really keep.

Help me see with eyes of faith;
give me strength to run this race.

I will go, Lord, where Your glory is unknown.
I will live for You alone.
I will go because my life is not my own.
I will go. I will go. I will go.

Notes from Your Journey

Notes from Your Journey

Notes from Your Journey

"The LORD bless you and keep you;
the LORD make his face shine upon you
and be gracious to you;
the LORD turn his face toward you
and give you peace." —Numbers 6:24–26

To find out more about Hannah's therapy
or
to order more copies of this book
visit www.intentionalparents.com.

Printed in the United States
17691LVS00001B/223-240